Stock Cars

Jesse Young

Illustrated with photographs
from NASCAR

Reading consultant:
John Manning, Professor of Reading
University of Minnesota

Capstone Press
M I N N E A P O L I S

Printed in the United States of America.

Capstone Press • 2440 Fernbrook Lane • Minneapolis, MN 55447

Editorial Director   John Coughlan
Managing Editor   John Martin
Copy Editor   Gil Chandler

Library of Congress Cataloging-in-Publication Data

Young, Jesse, 1941-
    Stock Cars / by Jesse Young.
        p. cm. -- (Cruisin')
    Includes bibliographical references and index.
    ISBN 1-56065-223-3
    1. Stock car racing--United States--Juvenile literature.
    2. NASCAR (Association)--Juvenile literature. [1.Stock car racing. 2. NASCAR (Association)]   I. Title. II. Series.
    GV1029.9.S74Y68   1995
    796.7'2'O973--dc20   94-26940
                                                                            CIP
                                                                            AC

ISBN: 1-56065-223-3

99 98 97 96 95   8 7 6 5 4 3 2 1

Table of Contents

Chapter 1

A Look at Stock Car Racing

It's a sunny day at the speedway. Brightly painted cars race on a track of hot, black pavement. You're not watching the action. You're watching the time clock on the scoreboard and your car in the pit area.

Your crew hurries to finish work on the car. They check tire pressure and front-end alignment. The newcomer on the team runs back and forth to the fence. He watches for the yellow flags that will slow down the race.

As crew chief, it's your job to keep the car running for the driver throughout the race.

Today, on the sixth lap, two cars spin out just ahead of your driver. There's the noise of scraping metal. Your car loses a quarter panel and a bumper.

That's how it is in stock car racing. It's about luck, skill, a good car, and a good crew. You need them all to win.

Chapter 2
The Start

Stock-car racing is now a big-time sport. It involves thousands of professionals and millions of dollars in prize money. But it wasn't always this way.

It all started in the South, in the 1930s, during **Prohibition**. In those days, some people brewed illegal whiskey in backyard **stills**. To get the whiskey to the customer, **bootleggers** needed fast drivers.

These drivers had to go faster than the government agents who chased them. To make the fastest cars possible, bootleggers modified their machines. A good bootlegging car could

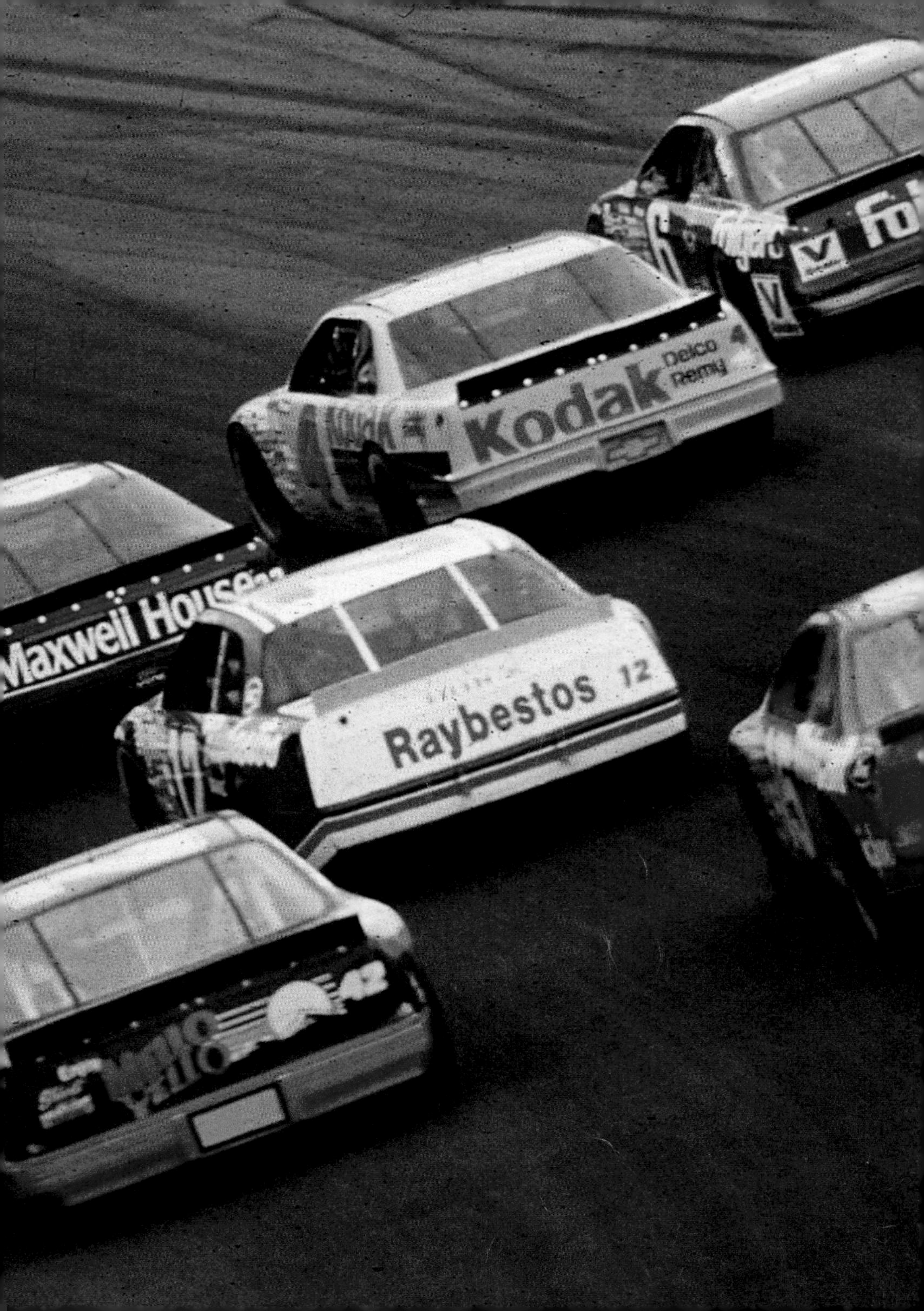

Kodak
Delco Remy
Maxwell House
Raybestos
12

accelerate to 95 miles (153 kilometers) per hour in first gear, 115 miles (185 kilometers) in second. Police cars could never go faster than 95 miles (153 kilometers) per hour.

Bootleggers also invented the "bootleg turn." When chased, they would spin around and take off in the opposite direction. If the police caught up with them, it meant jail. But if their modified cars worked the way they were supposed to, the bootleggers would escape.

Stock Cars in Cow Pastures

The bootleggers used to argue about who had the fastest car. They settled these disagreements by meeting to race in cow pastures.

The very first bootleggers' race took place in 1937 in Stockbridge, Georgia, about 15 miles (24 kilometers) from Atlanta. The racers

Skilled stock car drivers have to fight for position on a crowded track.

Stock car racing has gone from dirt tracks in cow pastures to the multi-million-dollar Daytona Speedway.

drove around a half-mile (.8 kilometer) oval until their tires had worn the dirt into a smooth track. They bet on the car they thought was fastest. Some even bet against their own cars.

At the next race, the crowd doubled in size, and at the next one it tripled. Soon bootleggers were racing every Sunday.

Modifying the Cars

In the beginning, stock car owners used junk parts to build their racers. They would put very large engines into lightweight cars. The slower cars the government agents drove were no match for these **modified** cars.

The speed and power of these new modified cars made stock car races even more exciting and popular. In a very short time, stock car racing would become a big-time sport.

Chapter 3

Bill France and NASCAR

Racing at Daytona Beach, Florida, started in 1936. At that time, an auto mechanic named Bill France organized a race along the sand. Bill told his friends to bring their cars down to the beach for a race.

The route ran along the beach and back down a stretch of oceanside road. The fastest car over this course would be the winner.

France took fifth place. He was a good mechanic and he had also worked on the winning car.

"Stock" Cars Only

The drivers could only use a "stock" car. A stock car was one that was left just as it came from the factory. Only safety features could be added.

The Automobile Association of America (AAA) sponsored the Beach Road race in 1936. The Elks Club put on the race the next year. Both organizations lost money on the races. Bill France could see that while there were problems in the business of stock car racing, there were also possibilities.

In 1938, some Daytona businessmen came to see France at his gas station and garage on Main Street. One of the men offered to put up the money for the race if Bill would organize it. Bill agreed. Promoting stock car races has been his work ever since.

NASCAR

In December 1947, Bill started an organization for stock car racing. He met with racers, mechanics, and promoters at the Streamline Hotel in Daytona Beach. At this

meeting, they organized the National Association for Stock Car Racing, or NASCAR.

"There are three reasons why NASCAR has succeeded," says Bill France proudly. "First, we have a point system that gives the racers credit for what they have done. Second, we have rules for the size and power of the cars, which keeps the races fair. Third, the cars are as safe as possible."

From the beginning, only cars from the United States have been allowed to race. Bill France thought that race fans wanted to see cars that were like the cars in their own driveways at home. He was right. The fans rooted for their favorite cars, and the races drew huge crowds.

"One of the reasons for stock-car racing's success," says Bill France, "is that ordinary people can understand the cars."

The Daytona track, built on the site of the first organized stock car races, was the world's largest racing speedway when it was finished in 1959.

The Tracks

Bill France always thought that stock-car racing needed its own special track. In 1950, the first asphalt superspeedway opened at Darlington Raceway in South Carolina. The crowds filled Darlington for the new NASCAR Grand National race. The Grand National **circuit** was off and running.

But France still wanted a better track—one that was exactly right for stock cars. He wanted to build it at Daytona Beach. The track would have steep banks so that cars could pass at high speeds in the turns.

After years of work and planning, France saw his dream come true. The 2.5-mile (4-kilometer) track, the largest speedway in the world, was completed in 1959. The track brought stock car racing out of the cow pastures of the 1930s.

If you visit the track at Daytona Beach today, you will see that each section carries a name. These are the names of great drivers who were killed while racing stock cars. They include Little Joe Weatherly, Fireball Roberts, and Bob and Fonty Flock.

In 1969, NASCAR built a superspeedway in Talladega, Alabama. At 2.66 miles (4.3 kilometers) Talladega's track is a little longer than Daytona's. It also has steeper banks than Daytona.

Pit crews have to work fast and get their tasks finished in a matter of seconds.

Technology

Over the years there have been few changes in stock cars. Although the drivers now use mid-size instead of full-size cars, the **wheelbase** is only a few inches shorter. The cars all weigh about 3,500 pounds (1,587 kilograms). Stock cars still look big and boxy like passenger cars.

"Stock" means that the car is just the way it was when it came from the factory. Although a stock-racing car may *look* like your own Chevrolet or Pontiac, there really is nothing "stock" about these machines. They must be exactly the same size as street models. But they're completely different under the hood.

Chapter 4

Inside the Cars

What's it like to ride in a stock car? It's hot! The oil lines and **exhaust** create a lot of heat. The temperature in the driver's seat can reach 140 degrees Fahrenheit (60 degrees centigrade). Drivers can sweat off ten pounds (4.5 kilograms) during a race. Some of them wear special suits and helmets that have cool water flowing through them.

It's loud as well. Even though drivers wear earplugs, a revved-up engine makes a tremendous noise. The drivers have to listen

Driver Dale Jarrett climbs into his stock car.

closely to their cars, so they can hear if a part breaks.

Driving a Stock Car

Drivers depend on their cars and especially on their brakes. As they charge toward a wall at full speed, they apply the brakes at the last second.

The stock-car driver uses the left foot on the brake. He uses the right foot to give the car gas while braking. That way, the car always stays in high gear. The driver usually changes gears only when going into or away from the pits.

Noise, heat, and danger are all a part of everyday life for stock-car drivers. They get used to hitting each other's fenders, dropping wheels, and spinning across the track.

Chapter 5

Getting the Most Out of the Car

There are many tricks of the trade in stock-car racing. Skilled drivers know how to get the most out of their cars–and out of their opponents.

Drafting

An important technique in stock-car racing is **drafting**. It follows the principle that two cars move through the air better than one.

Why? As the front car pushes through the air, it creates a **vacuum** in the space behind it.

The checkered flag comes out for the winner of the Daytona 500, stock car racing's premiere event.

When a second car moves into the vacuum, both cars go faster. This is because together the two cars are more **aerodynamic**. They can move through the air faster than a single car.

Bumping

Bumping other cars often occurs in stock-car racing. Some drivers do this to get an advantage over inexperienced drivers. Drivers will pull up behind a car and bump it. This sometimes causes the car being bumped to **fishtail** out of control.

When Cars Have Accidents: Yellow Flags

Drivers have to watch for waving caution flags. Caution flags make stock car races safer. When there is an accident and cars are blocking the track, an official waves a yellow flag. This means that the drivers must slow down.

It usually takes about six laps' time to clear the track or to clean up water, oil, or debris.

Chapter 6

Stock Car Racing Rules

In the early days, stock-car racers could race whatever cars they brought. Later, NASCAR set up some rules about cars. Today, each racing circuit, such as the Winston Cup circuit or the Grand National circuit, has certain specifications that the cars must follow.

The Winston Cup is NASCAR's top circuit. Grand National is second. Until 1984, Winston Cup and Grand National ran the same races.

To race in the NASCAR Winston Cup circuit, your car must meet detailed specifications. Here are some of them:

- Winston Cup racing is open to American-made, two-door passenger automobiles made in the last two years.

- The bodies must have hoods, fenders, bumpers, and grills.

- The doors must be covered with aluminum on the inside. They also must be welded to fender and quarter panels.

- The maximum **displacement** of the engines is 358 cubic inches (5869 cubic centimeters). Small-block **V-8 engines** must have standard measurements. Aluminum blocks are not allowed.

- Transmissions must be standard four-speed production transmissions.

- The wheelbase must be 110 inches (279 centimeters).

Chapter 7

Cars and Drivers Today

Safe cars, skilled drivers, and unbelievable speed are the keys to NASCAR's success.

Stock-car audiences today are the largest of any motor sport. There are always at least 150,000 people at the Daytona 500. More than three million people attend Winston Cup races each year. Over 170 million people watch these events on television.

"King" Richard Petty ruled stock car racing for many years before he retired in 1992.

Drivers race about 50 times a year, sometimes three times a week. Most drivers in other kinds of automobile racing get their start in stock car racing. Some, like Richard Petty, stay with stock cars for their entire careers.

"King" Richard Petty is the greatest stock-car driver of all time. In more than 1,000

Richard Petty

races, he collected 200 victories, including seven national championships. At his last Winston Cup race in 1992, he was named the grand marshal of the race.

Glossary

aerodynamic–a streamlined shape designed to cut smoothly through air resistance

bootleggers–people who make, sell, or transport alcoholic beverages illegally

circuit–an association of teams, clubs, or arenas that is organized for competition

displacement–the volume displaced by the pistons of an engine in moving back and forth

drafting–a method of following a car to more easily pass through the air

exhaust–the release of waste air or fumes from the engine

fishtailing–to swing the rear end of a car as a fish swings its tail

modify–to change the form or character of something

Prohibition–the period from 1920 to 1933 when the sale of liquor was not permitted in the United States

still–a vessel for heating liquids and condensing the vapors to make alcohol

V-8 engine–an engine with eight pistons arranged in a "V" formation of four pistons per side

vacuum–a space that is empty of air

wheelbase–the distance from the front to rear wheel in inches or centimeters

To Learn More

Dregni, Michael. *Stock Car Racing*. Minneapolis: Capstone Press, 1994

Olney, Ross R. *How to Understand Auto Racing*. New York: Lothrop Lee & Shepard Books, 1979.

Stephenson, Sallie. *Winston Cup Racing*. New York: Crestwood House, 1991.

Wilkinson, Sylvia. *Trans-Am*. Chicago: Childrens Press, 1983.

You can read articles about stock cars in two magazines: *Stock Car Racing* and *Hot Rod*.

Some Useful Addresses

**Canadian Automobile Sports Clubs Inc./
Fédération canadienne du sport automobile**
693 Petrolia Road
Downsview, ON M3J 2N6

International Motor Sports Association (IMSA)
P.O. Box 10709
Tampa, FL 33679

National Association for Stock Car Racing (NASCAR)
1801 Volusia Avenue
Daytona Beach, FL 32120-2875

Pro Stock Owners Associaton (PSOA)
155 E. Broad Street., 19th Floor
Columbus, OH 43215

**Modified Owners and Drivers Corporation for
the Advancement of Racing (MODCAR)**
363 N. Church Road
Wernersville, PA 19565

Index

Acknowledgments

A special thanks to NASCAR for photo assistance and to Dan Cunningham for his help with technical information.